Cool DIPS & DRINKS

Easy & Fun Comfort Food

ALEX KUSKOWSKI

Checkerboard Library

An Imprint of Abdo Publishing
www.abdopublishing.com

www.abdopublishing.com

Published by Abdo Publishing, a division of ABDO, PO Box 398166, Minneapolis, Minnesota 55439. Copyright © 2015 by Abdo Consulting Group, Inc. International copyrights reserved in all countries. No part of this book may be reproduced in any form without written permission from the publisher. Checkerboard Library™ is a trademark and logo of Abdo Publishing.

Printed in the United States of America, North Mankato, Minnesota
102014
012015

THIS BOOK CONTAINS
RECYCLED MATERIALS

Editor: Liz Salzmann
Content Developer: Nancy Tuminelly
Cover and Interior Design and Production:
Colleen Dolphin, Mighty Media, Inc.
Food Production: Frankie Tuminelly
Photo Credits: Colleen Dolphin, Shutterstock

The following manufacturers/names appearing in this book are trademarks: Gold Medal®, Krinos®, Oster®, Osterizer®, Proctor Silex®, Pyrex®

Library of Congress Cataloging-in-Publication Data
Kuskowski, Alex., author.
  Cool dips & drinks : easy & fun comfort food / Alex Kuskowski.
     pages cm. -- (Cool home cooking)
  Audience: Ages 7-14.
  Includes index.
  ISBN 978-1-62403-501-2
1. Cooking (Relishes)--Juvenile literature. 2. Fruit drinks--Juvenile literature. 3. Beverages--Juvenile literature. I. Title. II. Title: Cool dips and drinks.
  TX815.K87 2015
  641.81'2--dc23
                    2014024345

SAFETY FIRST!

Some recipes call for activities or ingredients that require caution. If you see these symbols, ask an adult for help.

HOT STUFF!
This recipe requires the use of a stove or oven. Always use pot holders when handling hot objects.

SUPER SHARP!
This recipe includes the use of a sharp **utensil** such as a knife or grater.

CONTENTS

DIP INTO COOKING!

Want to make tasty **refreshments** for friends and family? Whipping up dips and drinks is a great way to start! They are quick and easy. You can serve them up hot or cold.

Cooking food at home is healthy and tasty. It can be a lot of fun too. Many canned or frozen foods include unhealthy ingredients. When you make the food, you know exactly what's in it. It's easy to make a dish that's **unique** to you. Cook a recipe just the way you like it. Add fresh ingredients to make flavors pop. You can even share what you make with others.

Put the flavor back in your food. Start making home-cooked meals! Learn how to serve up some tasty dips and drinks for your next meal. Check out the recipes in this book.

THE BASICS

Get your cooking started off right with these basic tips!

ASK PERMISSION

Before you cook, ask **permission** to use the kitchen, cooking tools, and ingredients. If you'd like to do something yourself, say so! Just remember to be safe. If you would like help, ask for it! Always get help when you are using a stove or oven.

BE PREPARED

Be organized. Knowing where everything is makes cooking safer and more fun!

Read the directions all the way through before you start. Remember to follow the directions in order.

The most important ingredient of great cooking is preparation! Make sure you have all the ingredients you'll need.

Put each ingredient in a separate bowl before starting.

BE SMART, BE SAFE

Never work at home alone in the kitchen.

Always have an adult nearby for hot jobs, like using the oven or the stove.

Have an adult around when using a sharp tool, such as a knife or grater. Always be careful when using them!

Remember to turn pot handles toward the back of the stove. That way you avoid accidentally knocking them over.

BE NEAT, BE CLEAN

Start with clean hands, clean tools, and a clean work surface.

Tie back long hair so it stays out of the food.

Wear comfortable clothing and roll up long sleeves.

COOL COOKING TERMS

HERE ARE SOME HELPFUL TERMS YOU NEED TO KNOW!

CUBE / DICE

Dice and *cube* mean to cut something into small squares.

BOIL

Boil means to heat liquid until it begins to bubble.

DRAIN

Drain means to remove liquid using a strainer or **colander**.

CHOP

Chop means to cut into small pieces.

MASH

Mash means to press down on food with a pastry blender or potato masher.

MINCE

Mince means to cut or chop into very small pieces.

PUREE

Puree means to mix something in a blender until it is liquid.

MIX

Mix means to stir ingredients together, usually with a large spoon or electric mixer.

SHRED

Shred means to tear or cut into small pieces using a grater.

PEEL

Peel means to remove the skin, often with a peeler.

SPREAD

Spread means to make a smooth layer with a **utensil**.

COOL TOOLS

HERE ARE SOME OF THE TOOLS YOU WILL NEED!

aluminum foil

baking sheet

basting brush

blender

cutting board

electric mixer

measuring cups

measuring spoons

mixing bowls

mixing spoon

pastry blender

peeler

pitcher

saucepan

serving glasses

sharp knife

strainer

COOL INGREDIENTS

HERE ARE SOME OF THE INGREDIENTS YOU WILL NEED!

all-purpose flour

apples

blueberries

brown sugar

cheddar cheese

chocolate chips

chunky salsa

cilantro

cocoa powder

cranberries

garbanzo beans

garlic

green onions

guacamole

jalapeño

mangos

maple syrup

milk

Monterrey Jack cheese

pepper Jack cheese

pita pockets

red pepper

refried beans

sour cream

strawberries

tahini

tomatillos

tomatoes

white onion

CREAMY CHEESE DIP

Dig into some tasty melted cheese!

 MAKES 6 SERVINGS

INGREDIENTS

1 pound white American cheese

4 ounces Monterrey Jack cheese

½ cup half-and-half

1 tablespoon butter

¼ cup chopped white onion

½ teaspoon garlic powder

½ teaspoon onion powder

½ teaspoon cayenne

¼ cup cilantro (optional)

4 cups corn chips

TOOLS

measuring cups

measuring spoons

cutting board

sharp knife

medium saucepan

mixing spoon

serving bowl

pot holders

1. Cut the American cheese into 1-inch (2.5 cm) cubes. Shred the Monterrey Jack cheese.

2. Put the cheeses, half-and-half, and butter in a saucepan. Heat over low heat, mixing until the cheese melts. Take the saucepan off the heat.

3. Add the onion, garlic powder, onion powder, and cayenne to the saucepan. Stir well.

4. Pour the dip into a bowl. Sprinkle the cilantro on top for a pretty pop! Serve with corn chips.

TIP

Chop up a jalapeño pepper and add it with the onion for a spicy kick!

DAZZLING BERRY DRINK

Sip a fun fizzy drink!

1. Chop the strawberries into small pieces.

2. Put the strawberries, blueberries, lemon juice, and sugar in the blender. Puree the mixture until smooth.

3. Add the soda water to the blender. Mix on low until the ingredients are combined.

4. Fill glasses with ice. Pour the berry mixture into the glasses. Top the glasses with fresh mint.

 MAKES 4 SERVINGS

INGREDIENTS

2 cups strawberries
2 cups blueberries
3 teaspoons lemon juice
8 tablespoons sugar
4 cups soda water
ice
fresh mint (optional)

TOOLS

measuring cups
measuring spoons
sharp knife
cutting board
blender
serving glasses

HUMMUS DIP & PITA CHIPS

This combo will really get the party going!

 MAKES 8 SERVINGS

INGREDIENTS

PITA CHIPS

8 pita pockets

½ cup olive oil

¾ teaspoon black pepper

1 teaspoon garlic salt

DIP

1 16-ounce can garbanzo beans, drained

4 tablespoons lemon juice

2 tablespoons tahini

3 cloves garlic

1 red pepper, chopped

½ teaspoon salt

½ teaspoon black pepper

3 tablespoons olive oil

TOOLS

measuring cups

measuring spoons

baking sheet

aluminum foil

sharp knife

cutting board

mixing bowl

mixing spoon

basting brush

blender

serving bowl

pot holders

1 Preheat the oven to 400 degrees. Line the baking sheet with aluminum foil.

2 Split the pita pockets in half. Cut each pita circle into 8 triangles. Place the pita triangles on the baking sheet.

3 Combine the remaining pita chips ingredients in a mixing bowl.

4 Brush the oil mixture on the pita bread. Bake 5 minutes. Take the chips out and let them cool.

5 Put all the dip ingredients in the blender. Puree the mixture until smooth.

6 Pour the dip into a bowl. Serve it with the pita chips for dipping.

SUNNY MANGO COOLER

Sip a sweet mango drink!

1. Peel the mangos. Cut them in half and remove the seeds.

2. Cut the mangos into small cubes.

3. Put the mango, yogurt, sugar, and ice in the blender. Blend until smooth.

TIP
Try making a strawberry cooler! Replace the mangos with 2 cups of diced strawberries.

 MAKES 2 SERVINGS

INGREDIENTS
2 mangos
2 cups plain yogurt
½ cup white sugar
1 cup ice

TOOLS
measuring cups
peeler
sharp knife
cutting board
blender

SALSA VERDE SURPRISE

Bite into a sassy salsa that bites back!

  MAKES 4 SERVINGS

INGREDIENTS

10 tomatillos

2 garlic cloves, minced

1 cup chopped onion

2 jalapeños, chopped

1½ tablespoons chopped cilantro

1 tablespoon oregano

½ teaspoon allspice

1 teaspoon salt

2 tablespoons lime juice

¾ cup vinegar

TOOLS

measuring cups

measuring spoons

sharp knife

cutting board

saucepan

mixing spoon

blender

pot holders

1. Take the **husks** off the tomatillos. Wash and dice the tomatillos.

2. Put the tomatillos, garlic, onion, jalapeños, cilantro, oregano, allspice, salt, lime juice and vinegar in a saucepan.

3. Bring the mixture to a boil. Let it boil for 15 minutes. Take the mixture off of the heat.

4. Pour the mixture into a blender. Puree the mixture until smooth. Chill the dip 30 minutes in the refrigerator.

CRAN–APPLE PUNCH

Sour and sweet make the perfect drink!

 MAKES 4 SERVINGS

INGREDIENTS

1½ cups cranberries
⅓ cup brown sugar
4½ cups apple juice
¼ cup lemon juice
1 cup maple syrup
1 large apple, cubed
ice

TOOLS

sharp knife
measuring cups
pastry blender
mixing bowl
mixing spoon
strainer
pitcher

1. Put the cranberries, brown sugar, and ¼ cup water in a large bowl. Mash the cranberries with a pastry blender.

2. Add the apple juice, lemon juice, maple syrup, and 1¾ cups water. Stir. Make sure the sugar is completely mixed in.

3. Hold a strainer over the pitcher. Pour the cranberry mixture though the strainer into the pitcher. Chill the punch for 1 hour.

4. Before serving, add the cubed apple, some cranberries, and ice to the punch.

TIP
Add sparkling water with the ice and apple to make the drink fizzy!

SEVEN LAYER DIP

This dip has seven delicious flavors!

 MAKES 5 SERVINGS

INGREDIENTS

1-ounce package taco seasoning

16-ounce can refried beans

½ cup shredded pepper Jack cheese

½ cup shredded cheddar cheese

8 ounces sour cream

1 cup guacamole

2 tomatoes, diced

1 cup chunky salsa

1 cup diced green onions

tortilla chips

TOOLS

measuring cups

sharp knife

cutting board

mixing bowls

mixing spoon

measuring spoons

5 clear serving glasses

strainer

1. Mix the taco seasoning and beans together in a small bowl.

2. Mix the pepper Jack cheese and the cheddar cheese in a separate small bowl.

3. Put about 2 tablespoons of the bean mixture in each glass. Put 2 tablespoons of sour cream on top of the beans. Put two tablespoons of guacamole on top of the sour cream.

4. Put 2 tablespoons of chopped tomatoes on top of the guacamole in each glass. Drain the extra liquid out of the salsa. Put 2 tablespoons of salsa on top of the tomatoes. Put 2 tablespoons of the cheese mixture on top of the salsa.

5. Sprinkle green onions on top of the cheese.

6. Serve with tortilla chips for dipping.

BROWNIE BATTER SPREAD

Wrap up your homemade meal with a delicious dip!

MAKES 6 SERVINGS

1. Put the cream cheese and butter in a mixing bowl. Mix well with an electric mixer.

2. Add half of the powdered sugar. Mix well. Add the flour, cocoa powder, brown sugar, vanilla, salt, and 1 tablespoon milk. Mix until mostly smooth.

3. Add the rest of the milk and powdered sugar. Mix well.

4. Divide the dip between the serving bowls. Sprinkle chocolate chips on top. Serve with graham crackers.

INGREDIENTS

8 ounces cream cheese

6 tablespoons butter

2 cups powdered sugar

5 tablespoons all-purpose flour

5 tablespoons cocoa powder

3 tablespoons brown sugar

1 teaspoon vanilla extract

1 teaspoon sea salt

3 tablespoons milk

¼ cup chocolate chips

graham crackers

TOOLS

measuring cups

measuring spoons

electric mixer

mixing bowl

6 serving bowls

TIP

Try serving this spread with strawberries, apples, marshmallows, or pretzels!

CONCLUSION

This book has some seriously **delicious** dip and drink recipes! But don't stop there. Get creative. Add your favorite ingredients to the recipes. Make them your way.

Check out other types of home cooking. Make tasty breads, main dishes, soups, **salads**, and even **desserts**. Put together a meal everyone will cheer for.

WEBSITES

To learn more about Cool Home Cooking, visit booklinks.abdopublishing.com. These links are routinely monitored and updated to provide the most current information available.

GLOSSARY

colander – a bowl with small holes in it used to drain food.

delicious – very pleasing to taste or smell.

dessert – a sweet food, such as fruit, ice cream, or pastry, served after a meal.

husk – a thin, dry outer covering of a seed or fruit.

permission – when a person in charge says it's okay to do something.

refreshment – food or a drink.

salad – a mixture of raw vegetables usually served with a dressing.

unique – different, unusual, or special.

utensil – a tool used to prepare or eat food.

INDEX